MW00944566

Is Church "as is" Really Enough?

Prioritizing the Healing of God's People

Jeffrey V. Noble

All rights reserved. No part of this book may be reproduced or transmitted in any form or by any means without written permission from the author.

TheNobleTouch
TRANSCRIBING LIVES FOR OVER 20 YEARS

Is Church "as is" Really Enough?
Copyright © 2013 Jeffrey V. Noble

All rights reserved.

ISBN: 1482770865
ISBN-13: 978-1482770865

DEDICATION

I dedicate this book posthumously to my mother, Bernice Louise Noble, and my grandmother, Rebecca "Honey" Harrall, who introduced me to church and are now two of my ancestral angels. I just wish you were both here in the flesh so I could hug you.

ACKNOWLEDGMENTS

There are so many people to thank that I don't know where to start. Yes I do. This would not be possible without the guidance of my Lord and Savior Jesus Christ.

A special thanks to another ancestral angel, my martial arts instructor Grand Master Leon "Major" Wallace, who gave me discipline, self-esteem, determination and confidence; and showed me how to be a winner and overcome the odds. Karate was his religion.

I would also like to thank Rev. Dr. Johnny Ray Youngblood for his patience and for making himself available for this project. His challenging questions, yet supportive spirit, made this difficult subject easier for me to handle.

I also thank my New York Theological Seminary classmates/teachers. Although we did not always agree, you listened to my reasoning and logic.

In addition, I would like to give a special acknowledgment to my spiritual brother— the late Elder Robert Hooks.

Many thanks: to all of my students I've taught over the last 25 years; to The Noble Touch Empowerment Group, who keeps me accountable; and for the love and support of The Noble Touch Energy Healing Practitioners, whom God placed in my life to share and to love. You will never know how much you mean to me. When there was no one else I could talk to in my moments of weariness, you kept me going. You always came through for me no matter what I needed, especially Leslie Alston, Manuela Davis and Michelle Darden. You have been with me from the beginning. Oh yeah, you too Willy Legagneur (smile).

Thanks to the truly amazing: Denise Grant for computerizing the original handwritten manuscript, Yolanda McBride and Bentley Whitfield for proofreading and edits, and Jo Anne Meekins, "the pain," of Inspired 4 U Ministries for final edits and publication formatting.

Special thanks to the brilliant Angela Salgado and the countless ministers and pastors who took time to "spar" with me.

I also thank all my teachers in the field of personal development and self-help. There have been many. Some I met personally and some I only know through reading their materials. My teachers of Neuro-Linguistic Programming (NLP)— Richard Bandler, Robert Dilts, Tad James, Wyatt Woodsmall, Anthony Robbins and Christina Hall; My teachers of energy medicine— Masters Choa Kok Sui, Del Pe, and Glenn and Marilag Mendoza; and other teachers, whose books have inspired me— Brian Tracey, Zig Ziglar, Napoleon Hill, W. Clement Stone, T.D. Jakes, Michael Beckwith and Joel Osteen.

And final acknowledgements to my father James Noble Jr., who continues to demonstrate God's grace; my children Jeff and Ranah, who are the loves of my life; and my siblings James, Larry, Todd and Denise.

FOREWORD

There is no soul in the world like a critical lover. Reverend Dr. Martin Luther King Jr. epitomizes this in his life's call to urge America to live up to her promises and potential. All of the routes taken to awaken the nation from its coma of denial were necessary.

Jeffrey Vincent Noble, here in this initial work as well as in person, gives off the aura of being a critical lover of the church of Jesus Christ; especially the church in the black idiom— that social arena that has been the chief source of survival and hope for a people in pain based on pigmentation. The Black Church, though it has its history of both successes and failures, must continue under a keen critical eye ad infinitum. Each generation at least should bring to the table a spirit of inheritance and a sense of cutting edge urgency.

Jeffrey Vincent Noble does this with a hesitant boldness he feels necessity laid upon him to challenge, and to be capable and available.

To the open and the hungry, hear ye him!

While African-American, Jeff has had the experience of other cultures near and far; but, he has publicly announced on several occasions that his deep yearning was always to bring what he learned and experienced back home. Let's receive our son and brother.

Rev. Dr. Johnny Ray Youngblood,
Executive Pastor
Mt. Pisgah Baptist Church
Brooklyn, NY

CONTENTS

PREFACE

I was the kid from the housing projects in Harlem, N.Y. By society's standard, I wasn't supposed to amount to anything. I was voted "Class Clown" and "Least Likely To Succeed." I was led to believe that I did not deserve to be successful.

I was born to win, but conditioned to lose. However, we know that all things work together for the good of those who love God and are called according to His purpose (Romans 8:28).

God reconditioned me for success according to His purpose.

TheNobleTouch

"Before I formed you in the womb I knew [and] approved of you [as My chosen instrument], and before you were born I separated and set you apart, consecrating you; [and] I appointed you as a prophet to the nations." (Jeremiah 1:5, MSG)

INTRODUCTION

As a child, my mother and grandmother introduced me to the traditional Black Church. I had always been naturally inquisitive and in Sunday school, I would ask questions about God that went unanswered or completely ignored by the teacher. Eventually, I left church and went on to build a multi-million dollar business with the goal of educating, motivating and empowering African-Americans, who had limited opportunities.

I also began to seek out my own answers about God and spirituality. In my quest for helping others, I "discovered" several effective non-traditional methods of transforming lives rapidly. This was the beginning of my path in healing.

Over the past 30 years, I've been privileged to study healing modalities that are not widely known in the church, such as Neuro-Linguistic Programming (NLP), Pranic Healing, Meditation, and BeLife Sciences. Through these effective healing methods, I have treated and witnessed people liberated from phobias, release past hurts and emotional traumas and be relieved from chronic ailments. Lives were transformed in ways that were considered miraculous.

I returned to the Black Church in 1995 as a speaker, but eventually was led to join the congregation. I saw people who were in pain and suffering. How could I not share what I learned and had been practicing all those years outside of the "Church?" As Christians, aren't we called to be of service to our brothers and sisters? I soon realized that this unusual congregation, for the most part, was open to receive what I was gifted by God to share.

"For I was hungry and you gave me something to eat, I was thirsty and you gave me something to drink, I was a stranger and you invited me in, I needed clothes and you clothed me, I was sick and you looked after me, I was in prison and you came to visit me." (Matthew 25: 35-36, NIV)

This book was impregnated into my spirit in February 2010 at 4 a.m. while in India. I fought with God over many things that morning, including giving up a career that had been very good to me financially and professionally. My vision for writing this book is to have the Christian community partner with specialists in the field of transformation to create a more harmonious synergy between traditional prayer and the healing arts. I believe that the merging of these two powerful modalities (prayer and the alternative healing methods mentioned above) will create a more rapid and evident answer to many prayer requests. When combined with traditional prayer, these methods will increase the faith of most people.

Every Tuesday, although I don't speak Spanish, I work at a Senior Citizen center where the population is 99% Latino. The director of the program asked me to work one-on-one with a woman who had been in emotional pain since the tragic loss of her son in an accident over thirty years ago. Within thirty minutes, she released the pain associated to that tragedy. She is now able to think about her son and relive the happy memories without the pain of the tragedy. This Catholic mother had prayed thirty years for emotional relief to no avail until she was introduced to NLP, a practical healing modality.

For years in the traditional church, folks have been told to "pray, have faith, be good, and that the promise of a pain-free life is guaranteed to you in the hereafter. Prepare now to experience freedom in heaven. Suffering here on earth is noble. Sacrifice now so that you can have your treasures on the other side." We depend on our healing by having a Pastor, Minister, Deacon, Deaconess or Elder merely pray for us and anoint us. I contend that there are additional ways we can heal.

I usually get asked, "Is there a biblical basis for what you do?" Yes, the Bible clearly states that healing occurred in a variety of ways. For instance in 2 Kings 5, Naaman was healed of leprosy by his obedience to Elisha's instruction to wash in the Jordan seven times; in John 9, Jesus healed a blind man by making clay with His spittle, placing it on the man's eyes, and having him wash in the pool of Siloam; and in Acts 3, Peter told the lame beggar to walk in Jesus name, and took his hand and helped him up. The way we approach healing in some of our churches does not reflect the way that Jesus healed in the Bible or leave room for doing the "greater works than these" that Jesus spoke of in John 14.

TRADITIONAL THINKING: A BLESSING OR A CURSE?

Throughout the years, the Church has been the bedrock of the African-American community. It has become a hospital for all of our aches, pains and suffering. We have turned to the Bible for answers to our most pressing questions, for transformation of our lives, and for our salvation. We have been taught in church that "if we pray and have faith, God will answer our prayers" and "He may not come when you want Him, but He's always right on time." These clichés kept us and our parents full of hope.

As our world continues to evolve, we now have a new and younger generation, who has seen the sacrifice and suffering of their parents. This generation has seen their parents and grandparents attending church, being active in church, tithing in church and doing all the "right" things. They have also witnessed grandma suffering in pain on a hospital bed, and their parents barely making ends meet. Many are making the decision not to be devoted to church in the same manner as their parents and many are leaving the church. It is not that they do not believe in God or love God, but they are not feeling the same connection to the tradition of church.

Family, we are at a critical point in how we do "Church" and have to make some serious decisions. How are we going to equip believers with additional tools to respond to this ever-changing world? Are we going to conform to the ways of the traditional Church or are we going to renew our minds and create something greater? After all, it was Christ who said that we would do greater things than He. One way to help believers transform is to: *teach the application of the scriptures in a more practical way.*

****

Once upon a time there was a young bride who wanted to please her husband with a baked ham for their Sunday dinner. He watched as she unwrapped the ham and cut about 5" off the small end before scoring it, studding it with cloves, and basting it with brown sugar for baking.

Later as they enjoyed their meal, she eagerly asked him how he liked it. He made sure to rave about the ham first, but then asked, "I noticed that before you cooked it, you cut about 5" off the end. It seems a terrible shame to waste such a good ham, and I was wondering why you did that?"

"That's how you cook a ham," she asserted, but he pressed to know why. She could not tell him, but promised to ask her mother. When they spoke on the phone that afternoon she asked, "Mom, didn't you teach me to cut 4" - 5 " off the end of a ham before baking it? Why is that?"

*"Because that's just how you bake a ham,"
her mother replied. "That's how my mother
taught me. That's how we've always done it."*

*The new bride explained that her husband
was curious about the waste of good meat and
wondered why it must be done this way. The
mother promised to ask the grandmother the
next time they spoke.*

*That evening the mother called the
grandmother. "Mom," she said, "didn't you always
cut 4"- 5" off the end of a ham before baking it?"*

"Yes," the old grandmother said.

*"Why is that, Mom?" she asked, and the
grandmother replied, "Because my pan is too
short."*

******

Three generations of women had been
cutting the end off a ham because the
grandmother's pan was too short!

A major problem within most churches
is that they also want to keep doing things
the same way because that's how it's
been done for years. "But we have always
done it that way," is a familiar church
mantra. Many churchgoers have adapted
their parents' beliefs and customs about

God and the church without testing the relevance or validity for themselves. This dynamic illustrates embedded theologies or traditional thinking and raises the question, "A blessing or a curse?"

WHAT IS CHURCH?

I think a good place to start is with Webster's official dictionary definition. Church: (Noun) *a building used for public Christian worship, house of God, house of worship.*

Although the dictionary describes it as a building, scripture tells us that we, "the people," are the church. Without the people, there is no church. Which is true? For a lot of Christians, church is a building where people of the same religious beliefs go to worship, celebrate God, hear the Word, fellowship with friends, sometimes eat dinner and meet new people. They get encouraged, restored, rejuvenated, and renewed in their faith for another week by singing, praising and even dancing.

The early church, as recorded in Acts, was a social institution where resources were shared to meet the daily needs of the people. There was equal access to resources and people were empowered to perform miracles.

"They devoted themselves to the apostles' teaching and to fellowship, to the breaking of bread and to prayer. Everyone was filled with awe at the many wonders and signs performed by the apostles. All the believers were together and had everything in common. They sold property and possessions to give to anyone who had need. Every day they continued to meet together in the temple courts. They broke bread in their homes and ate together with glad and sincere hearts praising God and enjoying the favor of all the people. And the Lord added to their number daily those who were being saved." (Acts 2:42-47, NIV)

When we view church from a scriptural standpoint and believe the people are the church, it implies that each of us is a mini-church. If that is true, the question becomes, "If we are the church, then what is going on in our temples— the physical bodies?"

"Do you not know that your bodies are temples of the Holy Spirit, who is in you, whom you have received from God? You are not your own, you were bought at a price, therefore honor God with your bodies." (1 Corinthians 6:19-20, NIV)

So let's explore the concept that you are the church. How are you nourishing yourself? What are you doing to maintain your building? How are you constructing the building? What type of material are you reading for spiritual nourishment besides the Bible? How often do you meditate? What are some of your spiritual activities? How are you being of service?

"What goes into someone's mouth does not defile them, but what comes out of their mouth that is what defiles them." (Matthew 15:11, NIV)

A large majority of churchgoers attend church on Sunday only and are involved in very few outside activities that would build their spiritual muscles. What are you feeding yourself naturally (or is it spiritually)? Is it a diet of fear, doubt, worthlessness, victimization, helplessness, worry, hopelessness and poverty? How are you "pastoring" your inner church? What are you feeding the congregation of self? If you want the answer, seriously examine where you are right now in your life. Then you could also suppose that the title of this book be switched from *"Is Church 'as is' Really Enough?"* to *"Am I Really Enough?"*

Consider these question for yourself? What is the purpose of church to you? And is it really enough? When I sent out a survey to over 250 people, 92.6% of those who responded said, "No, Church is not enough." Yet every Sunday morning, all over the country, people flock to church as usual.

"What are people looking for when they go to church?" When this question

was asked, the most common answers from respondents were, "To hear God's word; to feel inspired; to feel good; to heal; and to worship God." Some even said that going to church was a habit or a tradition.

While all those things are true, what is clear is that "church" is not necessarily a transforming experience for them. In fact, most congregants have difficulty remembering what they experienced after leaving the church. When asked, some will remember that the choir sang really well or the beautiful piece the dance ministry performed. Or they may remember some catchy phrases from the preached word or the scripture reading. However, they cannot remember what biblical principle or spiritual practice was taught that can be applied to their daily lives because the quality of a sermon or service boils down to how good it makes them feel.

One respondent used the poem, "Why People Go To Church?" by an unknown author, to describe their thoughts about church:

Some people go to take a walk,
others go to laugh and talk,
some go there to meet a lover,
others go for their faults to cover.
Some go there to sleep and nod,
but few go there to worship God.

The past informs our present, which is why most churches still carry out the same traditions. Some church leaders are afraid of change or just don't know that there are other tools and effective healing methods available. They feel they may lose their congregations or lose their influence over them, but both Paul and Isaiah said to forget that which is behind and move forward into a new thing.

"Brothers and sisters, I do not consider myself yet to have taken hold of it. But one thing I do: Forgetting what is behind and straining toward what is ahead, I press on toward the goal to win the prize for which God has called me heavenward in Christ Jesus." (Philippians 3:13-14, NIV)

"Forget the former things; do not dwell on the past. See I am doing a new thing! Now it springs up; do you not perceive it? I am making a

*way in the wilderness and streams in the wasteland." (*Isaiah 43:18-19, NIV)

Each church has its own flavor. Some are politically oriented, some financially focused and some are about being "saved" from hell damnation; but very few churches are really focused on healing the people beyond the traditional prayer, anointing and fasting. Jesus was a healer and teacher. Shouldn't we, as the church, do what Jesus did?

"Whoever claims to live in him must live as Jesus did." (1 John 2:6, NIV)

Why aren't we taught how to develop a relationship with the Holy Spirit within us? Christianity, as it is being taught in some churches, has been stripped of its true Christ Consciousness. In most cases we are taught to always praise God outside ourselves, but very little is said about how to develop a relationship with the God within us. Interestingly enough, we accept the idea of the devil being inside of us and God being outside of us as someone we pray to from a distance. Yet, the Bible states that Jesus said He would ask the Father to send us a comforter, The Holy Spirit, who would live inside of us and teach us all things.

"And I will ask the Father, and He will give you another advocate to help you and be with you forever." (John 14:16, NIV)

WHAT DO YOU MEAN IS CHURCH REALLY ENOUGH?

For years the African-American community has depended on the church for healing, edification, strength, feeling good and a sense of community. Although there have been major social gains because of the political movements started in the Black Church by Black preachers, we have still fallen short of the type of transformation, personal growth, self-empowerment, true fulfillment and holistic healing available to believers. In addition, thousands of people, who have been praying for relief for decades, are still suffering with the same emotional and physical challenges.

Church, as we currently experience it, is not enough. Our churches of today may have newer and larger edifices, well-educated preachers, and state of the art technology in terms of sound systems and media equipment, but the condition of the people remains the same.

Are we using state of the art spiritual therapies to heal the people? Is a church service, prayer and anointing sufficient to transform a phobia, eliminate depression, remove anxiety attacks or overcome fear of success, failure and rejection? Does it help people heal faster? Will it get rid of emotional hurt and pain? Can it help people to forgive? The answer is "YES," sometimes or almost accidentally. So then, why is it that traditional methods transform negative feelings sometimes and not always? Is it that God liked the person better on Sunday than on Monday? Is it that God did not answer this prayer but answered the others? Does the measure of faith affect how prayers are answered or can you just have strong faith without prayer and still receive what you ask for?

I watched my mother, who was very involved with the church, pray for the cancer to be removed from her lungs only to lose the battle. Yet, there were other churchgoing people, who were considered mean-spirited but survived cancer. Why? I vividly recalled having those thoughts. When I found out that my mother had this disease, I prayed for her immediately. I also called members of my church, who prayed for her and put her name on the prayer wheel, but I did not use my training in healing modalities to help.

For two weeks, I would not work with my mother because I was afraid that if she died, my previous success with healing would be a fluke even though I had an 85% success rate with the people I had worked with. Then one night as I talked to God, I walked from my apartment in Harlem, past the corner bodegas, through Central Park and past all of the expensive shops in

Midtown Manhattan. The walk was about six and a half miles long, during which time I questioned why He would inflict my mother with such a deadly illness. She volunteered in the public school system to help underperforming students, attended church regularly, and also served and paid tithes. When I did not get an answer, I thanked God for using me as a vehicle for healing so many others, and continued to express concern for my mother.

That night I had an "Aha" moment and cut a deal with the Creator. The deal was that I would work with my mother if He guaranteed that she would not suffer in pain like my grandmother; and that she would be kept in her right mind while battling the illness or if she transitioned. If the Creator kept this covenant, I would continue to do the work as His vessel for divine blessings. I began to work with her consistently, using the alternative healing modalities throughout the next couple of months.

The afternoon before she transitioned, one of the ministers from my church came to the hospital. God used him to show me that in addition to honoring our covenant, He was also going to exceed what was promised. In my mother's hospital room, we prayed together, anointed her and served communion. She transitioned early the next morning, but I sensed a peace that she was fully prepared spiritually before she left her physical body. Throughout her battle with cancer, she had no pain at all and was always very conscious and alert. The covenant was fulfilled and I continue to keep my promise to be a vessel of healing and transformation to others.

I believe churches following Jesus Christ need to have a strong and effective healing ministry. When it comes to healing, most churches fall short. They talk about having a healing ministry, but it is limited to prayer, anointing, fasting, and traditional medicine. However, the people deserve more attention regarding their physical, emotional, mental and spiritual bodies.

There are some very powerful personal development, alternative healing and self-help modalities that will transform the lives of congregations faster and more effectively. These healing methods are currently used successfully outside of church; however, they can be utilized within the church to help heal the people along with prayer. In most cases, the church leadership is not aware of these methodologies, and in other cases, church leaders may feel uncomfortable about integrating these practices with church tradition. Finally, some church leaders may be open, but don't know where to start. That is why I am available to teach others, who are open, willing and ready to bring this life changing ministry to their communities and churches.

"Beloved, I pray that you may prosper in all things and be in health, just as your soul prospers." (3 John 1:2, NKJ)

****

One Woman's Personal Testimony

Since the day I was born, I have been in church. I have pictures of my mother and grandmother holding me at six weeks old in front of an urban store-front Baptist church. Over the past forty-five years of being in church, I've heard hundreds of preachers, speakers, deacons, evangelists, missionaries, and Sunday school teachers talk and teach about God / Jesus / The Holy Spirit and the dos and don'ts of being a Christian.

Like every person, I've had my share of ups and downs, which are a part of life. Has going to church helped me or empowered me to deal with life issues? When I was molested as a child and had feelings of guilt and shame as an adult, did going to church heal these wounds? When I got older and was involved in an emotionally abusive relationship, was going to church (praying, hearing a sermon, singing in the choir, ushering, going to Sunday service, tons of weekday revivals, going on church bus rides, etc.) healing to me? If I am truly honest, the answer would be "No."

I later discovered after years of "outside" therapy that my church activities were the mask I used to run away from my hurting self. It was the "drug" I used to fill the void of feeling inadequate. In church, I prayed to a God outside of myself; never was I taught about the God within myself. If asked, "Is church as we know it really enough?" My reply is "NO!" Or maybe it was enough to get me by week to week, which seemed good at that time.

Church has given me opportunities to release some emotional stress by hand clapping, shouting and screaming. Has it provided at times a shoulder to cry on, a warm embrace or a kind and encouraging word? Yes, but the core of the original problem (not feeling worthy and not connecting to the God-self) was still there. At times, I was even taught in church that I was unworthy and as filthy rag— something a woman in an abusive relationship didn't need to embrace.

I prayed for years and years that Jesus, the Savior, would set me free. When I discovered the Divinity within, my freedom journey began. I read books about achieving self-empowerment and enlightenment. I attended self-development workshops such as "Releasing The Past and Embracing the Future" that used NLP techniques that took me back to the root cause of issues doing timeline therapy to heal. We did deep inner healing meditations. In deep meditation, I connected to the God within and began learning to trust the God within me. I truly realized at that point that the kingdom of heaven was truly within me. Wow, so that's what Jesus meant! I *began to see the Jesus I had been taught about in a clearer "Light" and began to appreciate His work and teachings even more. I also began learning about the spiritual anatomy and other healing modalities. I discovered it was not a contradiction to my Christian faith, instead it helped to increase my faith. I saw biblical principles and teachings come alive in a most exciting way!*

****

RELIGIOUS CLICHÉS

I was talking to a friend about certain religious clichés. I told her that although the cliché "He may not come when you want Him, but He's always right on time" refers to God, it is oftentimes used as a copout. She got very upset and totally disagreed. I then reminded her of the time she was afflicted with very painful Carpal Tunnel Syndrome.

For two days, she was in pain and had been praying for help. I reached out to her to attend a healing workshop I was conducting called, "Releasing the Past and Embracing the Future." She said that she was in too much pain and preferred to stay home. I convinced her to come, promising that the pain would diminish. She came to the workshop, participated in the healing meditation and her pain was gone by the end of the workshop.

Do you think God was "right on time?" Suppose I did nothing to convince her to come? Some people may say that God used me as a vessel to persuade her. Suppose she had missed the workshop? If she still had the pain a week later, would that have been right on time? The point is that God could have answered a prayer several times before we received it, allowed it or recognized it. The time when we become aware of the answer is what Christians consider "right on time." Had I not been persistent, she could have missed the timelier blessing.

****

It had been raining for days and days, and a terrible flood had come over the land. The waters rose so high that one man was forced to climb onto the roof of his house to avoid the floodwaters, faithfully praying to God to save him.

As the waters rose higher and higher, a man in a rowboat appeared and told him to get in. "No," replied the man on the roof. "I have faith in the Lord, the Lord will save me." So the man in the rowboat went away. The man on the roof prayed for God to save him.

The waters rose higher and higher, and suddenly a speedboat appeared. "Climb in!" shouted a man in the boat. "No," replied the man on the roof. "I have faith in the Lord, the Lord will save me." So the man in the speedboat went away. The man on the roof prayed even harder, knowing that God would save him.

The waters continued to rise. A helicopter appeared and over the loudspeaker, the pilot announced he would lower a rope to the man on the roof. "No," replied the man on the roof. "I have faith in the Lord, the Lord will save me." So the helicopter went away. The man on the roof prayed again for God to save him, steadfast in his faith.

The waters rose higher and higher, and eventually they rose so high that the man on the roof was washed away, and alas, the poor man drowned.

Upon arriving in heaven, the man marched straight over to God. "Heavenly Father," he said, "I had faith in you, I prayed to you to save me, and yet you did nothing. Why?" God gave him a puzzled look and replied, "I sent you two boats and a helicopter, what more did you expect than that?" - Author Unknown

****

Another cliché that is widely used and also raises questions is: "It is just God's will" or "If it's God's will." Why do we bother to pray if God is going to do what he wants to do anyway? Is this cliché another way we can be passive and not take action? A pastor stated that prayer carries a reputation for changing God's will. What do you think? Is God's will unchangeable or does prayer change God's will? What do you have to pray in order for God to change His will and how do you know if His will is changed? Is it based on the answer you receive or the outcome of the situation?

CONSIDERATION FOR AN INTENTIONAL MINISTRY OF HEALING

It is often said that we are spiritual beings having a human experience, however, we are never taught what that means exactly. If we are spiritual beings, shouldn't we learn more about our embodied spiritual selves and the secrets to keeping them healthy and clean, strong and energized? Shouldn't we be taught how the spiritual body affects the physical body? Is it possible to help transform heart disease, diabetes, stress, anxiety and fears? How can we help our body heal itself?

"Jesus called his twelve disciples to him and gave them authority to drive out impure spirits and to heal every disease and sickness." (Matthew 10:1, NIV)

A medical doctor, in order to practice medicine, needs to know the anatomy of the physical body. Shouldn't those who are our church leaders know something about the spiritual anatomy and how we heal the spiritual body? What most people don't understand is that the problems that present themselves in the physical body start in the spiritual body. Our prayers are usually asking God to heal the physical ailment but not the spiritual cause of the problem.

It has been said that the church is a hospital and I can attest to a multitude of churchgoers, habitually attending church every Sunday, only to have the same ailments for 12, 15, and 20 years or more. If that is the case, then we need healers in the church to help the people. Are there enough "doctors" and "nurses" to service the people? Is it necessary to have a white uniform to qualify to be a doctor or a nurse? The answer is a resounding "NO!"

There are "Angels of Transformation" sitting in the pews of most churches, ready for the opportunity to serve and to help heal the people. Put out the call to meet with them, find out what methods they use. Research it and measure the effectiveness, then teach the people.

God used me to be a blessing to many people although I was outside of the traditional church. People's fears, phobias and past traumas were eliminated. The work was still ministry. I developed a personal relationship with God without being connected to a church building or organized religion. IT'S NOT ABOUT THE RELIGION, IT'S ABOUT THE RELATIONSHIP.

What other modalities are out there? Are you familiar with any of them? Why haven't different modalities of healing been introduced to the people? What do your people really want and how do you know if what you want for them is what they need?

Some Christians feel that they have a monopoly on gifts and that they are the only people that God can speak to. Could God have spoken to people of other faiths, other prophets and servants of God? The challenge of presenting new methods of healing to church leaders helps me to understand why there are so many wars over religion.

"Peter began to speak: 'I really understand now that to God every person is the same. In every country God accepts anyone who worships Him and does what is right." (Acts 10:34-35, NCV)

There are effective healing methods developed outside the traditional church that can help the church heal the people. God has given the knowledge to many people, therefore to believe that God only works within one religion or behind church walls is irrational. This type of thinking puts the church on a pedestal and God in a box. When pastors and other church leaders get on board with being open, they will be able to accelerate the speed of transformation in their congregations. Spirituality knows no boundaries.

"I revealed myself to those who did not ask for me; I was found by those who did not seek me. To a nation that did not call on my name. I said 'Here am I, here am I." (Isaiah 65:1, NIV)

As I began to share my gifts, skills and different healing modalities in the church, some were unwilling to accept the work because they did not understand it. Often I was asked, "What does this have to do with the Bible or with Jesus? Where did this stuff come from?" "Is this some New Age or Eastern Religion?" (By the way, Christianity is an Eastern Religion). An Elder in the church once told me, *"That kind of work has no place in the church."* I totally disagreed. Wasn't Jesus a healer? My response was, "If you see someone that is sick and suffering and you have medicine to give to that person, would you give it to them or decide not to because the medicine was not made in our city?"

What would Jesus do? He would heal the person! Jesus wasn't traditional. He broke tradition, putting those in need first. If we, as Christians, are following Jesus, who broke tradition, then why are a majority of churches stuck in traditional thinking?

"On a Sabbath Jesus was teaching in one of the synagogues, and a woman was there who had been crippled by a spirit for eighteen years. She was bent over and could not straighten up at all. When Jesus saw her, He called her forward and said to her, "Woman, you are set free from your infirmity." Then He put his hands on her and immediately she straightened up and praised God. Indignant because Jesus had healed her on the Sabbath, the synagogue leader said to the people, "There are six days for work. So come and be healed on those days, not on the Sabbath." The Lord answered him, "You hypocrites! Doesn't each of you on the Sabbath untie your ox or donkey from the stall and lead it out to give it water? Then should not this woman, a daughter of Abraham, who Satan has kept bound for eighteen long years, be set free on the Sabbath day from what bound her?" When He said this, all his opponents were humiliated, but the people were delighted with all the wonderful things He was doing." (Luke 13:10-17, NIV)

I understand the fear people have of the unknown; yet they walk around this world every day, utilizing things they don't understand, such as electricity. Jesus was a healer. If we were to take away the healing miracles of Jesus, we would have a great teacher. Transforming a person's life is biblical because that's what Jesus did.

Good leadership does not mean you have to know it all, but isn't it your responsibility to have the wisdom and discernment to identify and to introduce the resources that will help the people you serve?

THE RENEWED CHURCH

The Renewed Church must begin to focus on the development of the total person. The intention of church leadership must be on building people, not buildings; and building families and communities, not just membership. Only then will the true success of the church be based on how many lives are physically, emotionally, mentally and spiritually transformed.

"The God who made the world and everything in it is the Lord of heaven and earth

and does not live in temples built by human hands." (Acts 17:24, NIV)

If the Spirit of God dwells within us and we are all sons and daughters of God, why are we so controlled by our habits? Contemplate the idea of Divinity versus humanity. Why do we allow our humanity to have more control than our divinity? You would think it should be easy to break a habit if you activate the Spirit of God within you.

"It is for freedom that Christ has set us free. Stand firm, then, and do not let yourselves be burdened again by a yoke of slavery." (Galatians 5:1, NIV)

What we believe about ourselves has created the life we are living right now. We are all conditioned and programmed by our past. Why does past conditioning have more power than the Spirit of God that is within us? How do we begin to implement practices that increase our ability to tap into our inner divinity so that we can overcome and transform the things that block our success, happiness, joy and peace?

"So from now on we regard no one from a worldly point of view. Though we once regarded Christ in this way, we do so no longer. Therefore, if anyone is in Christ, the new creation has come: The old has gone, the new is here! 18 All this is from God, who reconciled us to himself through Christ and gave us the ministry of reconciliation: that God was reconciling the world to himself in Christ, not counting people's sins against them. And he has committed to us the message of reconciliation. We are therefore Christ's ambassadors, as though God were making his appeal through us. We implore you on Christ's behalf: Be reconciled to God." (2 Corinthians 5:16-20, NIV)

The Renewed Church emphasizes that we are all individual expressions of God and helps us reconnect with that divinity within ourselves.

"This is how we know that we live in Him and He in us: He has given us of His Spirit." (1 John 4:13, NIV)

We will come together to worship, hear and be taught how to live the Word, using practical methods. New applications and technologies are available for self-growth, self-healing and self-realization. Pastors and church leaders are the facilitators in teaching people to become self-sufficient in personal development and spiritual growth. Self-sufficient here does not mean "I do it all myself" in terms of vanity. Self-sufficient refers to teaching people to tap into the power of their own divinity.

As long as we continue to look for deliverance outside of ourselves, we will never be empowered. Additional ways to empower the self spiritually is through practices such as healing meditation, prayer, affirmations and self-development work. Remember the old adage, *"If you give a man a fish, he will eat for one day, but if you teach him how to fish, he can eat for a lifetime."*

Empowering individuals to embrace the truth of their divine identity and inheritance is Jesus' prayer:

"My prayer is not for them alone. I pray also for those who will believe in me through their message, that all of them may be one, Father, just as you are in me and I am in you. May they also be in us so that the world may believe that you have sent me. I have given them the glory

that you gave me, that they may be one as we are one— I in them and you in me—so that they may be brought to complete unity. Then the world will know that you sent me and have loved them even as you have loved me." (John 17:20-23, NIV)

"For those who are led by the Spirit of God are the children of God. The Spirit you received does not make you slaves, so that you live in fear again; rather, the Spirit you received brought about your adoption to sonship. And by Him we cry "Abba, Father." The Spirit himself testifies with our spirit that we are God's children." (Romans 8:14-16, NIV)

A wonderfully spirited woman, who attends my church, was diagnosed with Multiple Sclerosis (MS) but has not let it own her. She is very active and if she didn't tell you, you would think she was perfectly healthy. One day when she approached me and told me about her experience with MS, she asked had I ever worked with MS specifically. I told her, "No, but I would love the opportunity to work with you." Then, two of the Energy Healing Practitioners and I worked with her every week for four months and bi-weekly for an additional two months. She testifies of permanent relief from a 10 year physical pain that felt as if she'd been beaten in her back and body with a baseball bat and could lift only her head with any ease each morning prior to the treatments.

She also participated in the "Releasing the Past and Embracing the Future" workshop and felt an emotional load lifted. When I followed-up with her, she spoke of occasional minor discomfort but none of the severe pain from before. Why? It's because the MS was also linked to an emotional experience. Releasing the emotional experience through a healing meditation and an NLP personal timeline exercise, lessened the MS flare-ups which now only resurface in connection with occasional worry and stressful situations.

In addition, releasing past emotional traumas helped her tap into her divinity and draw closer to God, instead of giving into the illness.

NOTE: *This woman no longer exhibits the various symptoms associated with MS and was able to throw away a lot of her medication. She* *currently takes therapy (the injection) to stop the progression of MS and only keeps the medication refills as a backup for stiffness due to weather. Her doctor says she's doing very well.*

The Renewed Church will provide additional ways for members to connect to the Holy Spirit within and teach about building a relationship with that aspect of the self. The world would experience a big shift if churches taught that we are one with Divinity.

The Renewed Church will be a movement of people serving in the world to lift the human spirit to new levels of Christ-likeness, having the same love, being of one accord, and of one mind, which is the true kingdom of God.

"You are the light of the world; a city built on a hill cannot be hidden." (Matthew 5:14, NIV)

Jesus Christ prioritized healing in His ministry and the Renewed Church will follow in the footsteps of the Messiah. The Renewed Church will develop a very intentional healing ministry with certified practitioners who provide holistic services that partner with prayer and traditional medicine to create a synergetic approach to wellness.

For example, before members of the church go into the hospital for surgery, they will come to the Elders for prayer and anointing, and then receive an energy medicine treatment by a practitioner to prepare their bodies for surgery. Energy medicine is the science of using the natural energy fields that surround the body to enable the physical body to heal naturally. It is considered a new field in modern medicine, according to the U.S. National Center of Complementary and Alternative Medicine although energy healing has been around since the beginning of time. When the members come out of surgery or the hospital, they will be prayed for and anointed again, and receive follow-up energy treatments as needed.

I witnessed, on numerous occasions, reduced recovery times when this combined treatment is used. There are many cases where conventional medical professionals cannot identify the source of an illness someone is experiencing. Why? It is because the root cause of the illness is spiritual or emotional. Medical Science cannot detect this type of imbalance. Remember, we are spiritual beings having a human (physical) experience.

I pray every day that the leaders of churches will consider and be open to healing practices that produce additional positive results for their flock, and thus increase their faith and build a stronger body of Christ. If the people are not healed, it will be more challenging for them to become more Christ-like because their humanity and divinity will be compromised.

The Renewed Church will be a place for its congregation to go for various types of resources and complementary healing services. The healing ministry must be a vital ministry in the Renewed Church. I am not suggesting that the congregation avoid conventional medicine, but just the opposite. I am saying to continue to pray and go to your doctor to handle the symptoms; but in addition, let us work together on the spiritual self. This is the most powerful way to create healing in the physical, mental, emotional and spiritual bodies.

There are over 500 verses in the Gospel books of the Bible that tell about the healing ministry of Jesus Christ, as referenced in the article, "Healing In The Gospels" at—
http://www.voiceofhealing.info/02history/gospels.html.

By the way, how many scriptures can you find where Jesus just prayed for someone's healing?

Chapter 20 in The Gospel of John, noted that there were many other signs Jesus performed that were not written down.

Jesus was a healer, who made healing a priority. If we are to do what Jesus did, the church must make healing the people a priority now!.

A MESSAGE TO CHURCH LEADERSHIP

"Do not be conformed to this world, but be transformed by the renewing of your minds, so that you may discern what is the will of God— what is good and acceptable and perfect."
(Romans 12:2, NRS)

Using my imagination, I wondered what Paul would say to the Church today. I wondered whether the words he wrote to the believers in Rome while he was in Corinth, encouraging them not to conform to the ways of this world (age) but to transform by the renewing of their minds, would apply to the Church and how it would apply.

In the past 18 years since I returned to the Church, not much has changed. A significant number of Christians put all their faith in the Bible without really developing a relationship with the One who inspired it. A lot of suffering goes on unnecessarily because church leaders, for the most part, are operating from their embedded theologies and have not transformed their minds to imagine what else is available to transform and renew the minds of their congregations.

The Bible doesn't always indicate specific application. Let's look at an example. The King James Version of 2 Timothy 1:7 states, "The Lord has not given us the spirit of fear but of power, love and a sound mind." How many preachers teach practical methods of how to overcome fear? The church that begins to really make the scriptures come alive with practical applications will become a renewed church that really transforms lives rapidly.

We don't have to look far to see that teenage pregnancy is still an issue. There are also increased rates in unemployment, crime, drugs, incarceration and school dropouts while church attendance across the country has decreased. Our health care is on the decline and there are more stress related illnesses now than ever before. For most people in church, the hand clapping, singing and praise is just a band-aid approach to hold us until next Sunday's service.

Embedded theologies can be a curse when it prevents the people of God from receiving relief from that which ails them, and prevents leaders from seeing how God is using other people and methods. A church leader once told me that the healing modalities I practice should be done outside of the church. In other words, I should use God's gifts to help people just not inside the church building.

Why would a church leader say something like this? Jesus was a healer and transformed the lives of people. He hung out with the undesirables and He broke tradition. He was revolutionary. During seminary classes, I realized it was the embedded theology that influenced this church leader's statement. Imagine if Jesus had the same embedded theology as the synagogue ruler. He would have never healed on the Sabbath (Luke 13:10-17).

As a matter of fact, if Jesus showed up today, would we accept him based on our embedded theology?

Embedded theology that is based on traditional thinking does not allow one to be open to having a discussion to understand the gifts of others and how they can be used to help God's people. Scriptures like 1 Corinthians 12 tell us that God gives different gifts to different people and how these gifts are to be used to build the body of Christ.

It is this type of hypocrisy that causes the decline in our membership, especially among young people, and causes critical thinkers to leave the church to seek other means of spirituality. Jesus' theology was revolutionary, yet our churches today seem to be mostly focused on following traditions. Traditional embedded theology can make it challenging to develop a Christ-like mind.

The Church has the ability to let go of tradition and try something new. It has done so in the past. Let's look at dance in the church. It was probably only 30 years ago that dance, as we know it now, was not allowed in churches. You would be considered a sinner if you even went to a party. So surely dancing in church was not acceptable. But someone persevered and liturgical dancing is done all over the country although some people are still against it. The church renewed its mind and dance has been a blessing and another way of ministering and healing the people.

Let's look at singing. Although we love our traditional old school gospel songs, if it were not for Kirk Franklin and others who broke tradition, we would have lost a whole generation of young people. This new type of gospel allows our youth to relate the "Good News" to music, thereby renewing their interest in church. The church renewed its mind and it blessed our youth!

It's not that the church can't or hasn't stepped outside the box of embedded theologies. It just takes time. We have to allow God to do His will in the field of healing and transformation. That's what Jesus did and it was the part of His ministry that proved He was the Son of God. Everyone, from the oldest to the youngest saint in the church, can benefit from some type of transformational healing.

The rampant suffering in our own lives and neighborhoods behooves us to explore the proven methods used outside of the church that rapidly transform conditions. We need a healing revolution within the Church— a movement supported by church leadership that is dedicated to the transformation of our people and our communities.

Paul's letter to the believers in Rome is as relevant today as it was centuries ago. Believers were urged to transform by renewing their minds.

One day, in the depths of my meditation, I called out Paul's name and asked to speak to him. I told Paul that the Church is going through a crisis. I told him about the incarceration, unemployment, crime and teenage pregnancy rates in our community. I told Paul that our senior citizens are losing their homes and can't afford their medicine. I told him about the suffering of our people and the spiritual, emotional, physical and mental pain.

I said to Paul, "I know that when you wrote to the believers in Rome and told them not to conform to the ways of this world but to be transformed by the renewing of the mind, you meant through prayer, faith and obedience to God's Word. But Paul, that was thousands of years ago. Yes, we MUST have faith and stay in the Word of God. However, since then God has given people ideas, methods and processes to help us transform our thinking and renew our minds. Just like He gave Thomas Edison and Lewis Latimer the idea for an electric light; gave Albert Einstein the idea for relativity; gave Henry Ford the idea for a gasoline driven car; gave George Washington Carver hundreds of ideas for using a peanut; and gave Harriet Tubman the idea to transport the enslaved to freedom. Today, God is still giving other willing people ideas, methods and processes to transform people by the renewing of their minds."

"Paul, can I bring the gifts God has given me to the Church today? Can you write them a letter?" Then Paul told me to calm down because he saw the excitement and passion that God put in me about this work ... then he told me a story. It was about John, who saw a man casting out demons in the name of Jesus (Mark 9:38-41). He went back and told Jesus about what he saw and Jesus said not to stop him because no one who does a miracle in my name can in the next moment say anything bad about me. For whoever is not against us is for us.

Then Paul said to me "As long as you keep prayer and worship first, and you are transforming and renewing minds in the name of Jesus, I'll write the letter for you." Then he paused a moment and said, "My brother, they will read it, but will their embedded theology prevent them from acting on it?"

SURVEY RESULTS

The survey responses to the question, "Is church really enough?" resulted in 92.6% of the respondents saying, "No, church is not enough?"

Below are some of the responses to the follow-up question:

Why or Why not?

1. Most Christian churches (I am restricting my answer to Christian churches because I believe they are the emphasis of your book) are not enough because I think they do not place enough emphasis on the spiritual growth of the individual. For instance, how can you be a member of a church and be involved in the making or selling of alcohol

or cigarettes, come home and beat your wife, be broke, busted and disgusted or be involved in harmful actions, etc. All we have to do is take a look at how most people are living their lives in the United States to see that church is not enough.

2. Church is great! But, there are other aspects of spirituality that are not explored: such as active meditation and claiming the goodness of the Universe. We spend too much time talking to God opposed to letting God speak to us. We also do not pull from the other divine elements that could help us in our lives.

3. There are a lot of things you can use in your life that churches do not supply, but you can incorporate in your praise and worship.

4. Must have own PERSONAL relationship with GOD.

5. Church is for us to come together to hear God's word and to worship as a group. It's what we do when we are not in church that's more important. We must develop and nurture our individual relationship with God.

6. Because the doors are no longer open 24 hours 7 day a week; because people need encouragement, to be listened to, to know

that they matter. No one entity is enough, but the church could certainly go a long way to close the gap. If only they would.

7. Church for me is my foundation but I know that church as it is defined in this day and age can't give you everything you need. Church can or should offer you the space/ tools to grow your relationship with God, but that doesn't happen if you rely on church to do everything for you ... provide you with the script, examples, etc. God is not confined to church and some people can't see that. When you can only see God through the confines of the physical church, you lose the ability to really see God at work and connect with God on a higher level.

8. Sometimes I feel that people are being held back or not given the healings we as a people so desperately need.

9. Church keeps one flooded with the Word, however self awareness and self love is also needed to motivate and challenge us to conquer fear so that one can live in the now and stay focus on achieving our dreams to be successful in life. Church does not always grow the individual from the inside out.

10. The Bible has its place in history as all good and popular books do, but times have

changed. People need to learn about real people they can relate to and emulate, not fictitious characters.

11. No, Church is simply one institution. It needs to work in conjunction with other institutions in our society to bring about real change.

12. The church is enough for those who need to find their way, and the need is answered. But there is much more to life than just church alone. God would not have created this world with so many different types of people in and out of church communities if there was just one belief system.

13. It is enough because the church is in me. The question is am I doing everything that I am destined to do. Am I fulfilling the purpose that GOD said was written in the book of life. The church has all that it needs because every member has a purpose that they can only fulfill. Just like the heart cannot do without blood to function and the lungs cannot operate without oxygen. Thus one cannot operate without the other. When the church recognizes that it is to be a servant like Jesus healing, teaching and preaching, it will be more than enough.

14. I wanted to check both yes and no above and since I couldn't I want to elaborate by saying that church is enough for the limited

and controlled role it plays. Church is a religious institution based on individual beliefs and if people want additional religious instruction, they can go outside the church or study on their own for their own individual purposes. There will be times people will need to seek additional spiritual and religious development on their own - things most churches are not capable of providing.

15. What happens when you leave church, life goes on.

16. Too much entertainment and not enough information.

17. You have to fellowship and read the Word daily; you have to minister to the people around you so you can build Gods kingdom and spread His word.

18. Because there are a whole lot more to learn besides just going to church.

19. So many churches have limited scopes that don't allow for ALL of the ways that God provides to meet the needs of His people. Churches limit the avenues "allowed" for people to find the answers they are looking for. Fear based doctrine creates fearful, constricting responses to situations.

20. Church is the foundation training tool, to train the believer in the God of Abraham, as to how to live a life of service to the God of Abraham.

21. There is no need for church for me.

22. You can't keep yourself isolated from the world but we have to live in it.

23. I feel church serves as one part that can assist an individual as they work toward becoming whole.

24. We are admonished to practice God's principles in our homes and communities. We are to be aware of others who do not know as we are supposed to know, and share and bring those into the folds that do not know Him in the free pardoning of their sins.

25. Church isn't enough if it is focused purely on religious doctrine vs. the unity of mind, body and spirit and helping each soul to find and move toward its own divine destiny.

26. Church can guide you on your spiritual path; however communing with God/ Spirit is an individual/ personal experience. You have to be ready and you have to want to.

ABOUT THE AUTHOR

Jeffrey Vincent Noble is a Transformation Christian Life Coach and the leading Human Potential Engineer in the world. He is also one of the few practitioners that guarantees results from the first visit. His training and work in the Healing Arts and Sciences started in 1986 when he studied with the co-founder of Neuro-Linguistic Programming (NLP), Richard Bandler, and became a Certified NLP Master Practitioner/Trainer in 1988.

In 1994, Mr. Noble began studying Energetic Healing with the founder of Pranic Healing — Grand Master Choa Kok Sui and his top trainers — where he became an Energy Medicine Practitioner. In 2010, after studying and practicing in India, Mr. Noble was led to leave corporate America after 15 years and fully dedicate his life to healing, coaching, educating, motivating and empowering individuals and families in the community, the country and the world. Upon his return from India, Mr. Noble began training others and founded The Noble Touch.

Since Mr. Noble began healing work over 25 years ago, he has successfully helped people from all walks of life to free themselves of physical and emotional pains due to past traumas and stress related illnesses.

Mr. Noble has expertise in a variety of transformational healing modalities, including Neuro-Linguistic Programming (NLP), Energy Medicine, and Emotional Freedom Technique (EFT).

Although Jeffrey V. Noble has been featured as a successful entrepreneur in Black Enterprise Magazine, The New York Times, NY Daily News, and Chicago Defender among many other publications and media, his healing and coaching work have been a SECRET to the community at large for decades. His business acumen and healing gifts have also been covered on Fox 5 Good Day New York and the WPIX Entrepreneur Series. In addition, Mr. Noble was previously selected as an Outstanding Young Man of America in recognition of outstanding professional achievement, superior leadership ability and exceptional service to the community.

In the late 1980's Mr. Noble was the New York State Karate Champion and was ranked 9th in the world in full-contact kickboxing. But, God had another plan.

Who would have thought that hands once used to hurt others in a professional sport would be transformed into hands that heal.

TheNobleTouch

TRANSFORMING LIVES FOR OVER 30 YEARS

Transforming Lives Through Coaching and Healing:

The Noble Touch provides a prayer-centered holistic approach to health and wellness. This method is a no touch – no drug – no side effect treatment. It is a natural and alternative way to improve your physical, spiritual, mental and emotional well-being by eliminating stress.

Did you know that the medical community states that 85% of all major illnesses are stress related? Imagine the stress of life and years of emotional baggage just melting away in one 45 minute session. This amazing experience will rejuvenate your mind, body, and spirit. Your essence will come alive and your body will begin to heal itself.

The power to affect the health and wellness of YOU and YOUR family is within your reach. Reach out to The Noble Touch to learn how to benefit from and access this transformative information.

Healing Services

Through coaching and healing, several of the conditions treated by our certified practitioners are included on but not limited to the list below:

- Unforgiveness, Anger, Fear, Shame, Guilt, Stress, Anxiety, and Depression
- Problems of the Reproductive System
- Gastrointestinal Ailments
- Pain Relief from Menstrual Cramps, Migraines, Arthritis, Lower Back
- Respiratory System
- Cancer and HIV
- Alzheimer's and Dementia

Remote Healing Services
(available for all conditions)

Also

Free Monthly Community Nights of Healing
(Stress-Relief Sessions)
Every 1st and 3rd Monday @ 7 p.m.
Bedford Stuyvesant Restoration Plaza
1368 Fulton Street, Ste. 519, Brooklyn, NY 11216

Workshops and Trainings

- Releasing Your Past and Embracing Your Future
- New Secrets to Achieving Your Goals and Living Your Dreams
- What Everyone Over 40 Should Know About Attracting the Ideal Mate
- How to Eliminate Mental Parasites
- Take Your Power Back: Forgiving and Letting Go
- The Twin Towers that Guarantee Success

For more information about speaking, coaching, healing or workshops and trainings, please contact **Jeffrey V. Noble** at:

877-493-9433, ext. 700

Or
info@thenobletouch.com

Or
http://www.thenobletouch.com

*Visit our website and **sign up now** for our FREE Monthly Transformation Tele-Conferences on the 1ˢᵗ and 3ʳᵈ Sunday @ 8 p.m. EST*

19162699R00047

Made in the USA
Charleston, SC
09 May 2013